LEARNING MATERIALS CENTER
SYLVIA ANGEL, DIRECTOR

Dinosaurs

WONDER
STARTERS

Dinosaurs

Pictures by LAURENT SAUVEUR SANT

Published by WONDER BOOKS
A Division of Grosset & Dunlap, Inc.

51 Madison Avenue New York, N.Y. 10010

About Wonder Starters

Wonder Starters are vocabulary controlled information books for young children. More than ninety per cent of the words in the text will be in the reading vocabulary of the vast majority of young readers. Word and sentence length have also been carefully controlled.

Key new words associated with the topic of each book are repeated with picture explanations in the Starters dictionary at the end. The dictionary can also be used as an index for teaching children to look things up.

Teachers and experts have been consulted on the content and accuracy of the books.

Published in the United States by Wonder Books, a Division of Grosset & Dunlap, Inc.

ISBN: 0-448-09660-9 (Trade Edition)
ISBN: 0-448-06380-8 (Library Edition)

PRINTING 1972

Printed and bound in the United States.

This is a dinosaur's skeleton.
Dinosaurs lived long, long ago.

Long ago the world looked different.
There were no people.
The plants were different.

The animals were different.
Some of the animals were dinosaurs.
There were different kinds of dinosaurs.

Some dinosaurs were small.
This one ate other animals.
It was a meat eater.

This dinosaur was very big.
It was a plant eater.
It walked on four legs.

The big dinosaur was very heavy.
Sometimes it stood in the water.
The water helped it to stand.

This dinosaur ate plants.
It had spikes on its tail.
The spikes helped it fight.

This dinosaur had a collarbone.
It had horns on its head.
The horns and collarbone
helped to keep it safe.

This dinosaur was very tall.
It walked on two legs.
It ate other dinosaurs.

The tall dinosaur had a big head.
It had lots of sharp teeth.

This dinosaur ate plants and trees.
It stood on its back legs.
Each foot had three toes.

There were other animals, too.
They were not dinosaurs.
Some flew in the air.

Some swam in the water.

This dinosaur died by a lake.
It fell down in the mud.

It became a skeleton.
After a long time,
the mud covered the bones.

The mud slowly turned into rock.
The bones turned into fossils.

After a long time,
the rocks were pushed up.
The fossils came to the top again.

Scientists look for fossils in rocks.
They found the fossil dinosaur bones.
They took the fossil bones from the rocks.

They took the fossil bones to the museum.
They put the bones together.

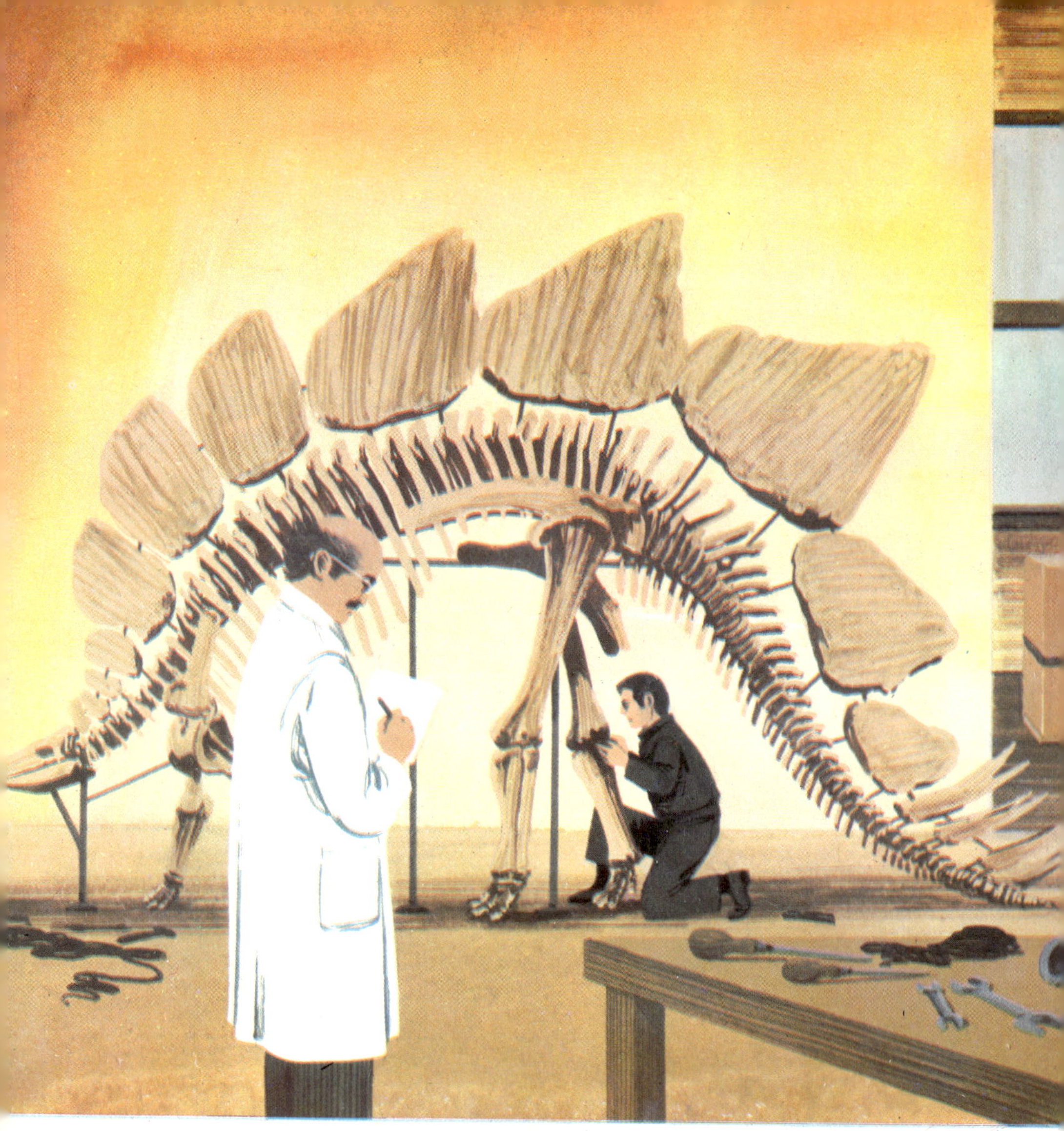

The scientist made the skeleton again.
It shows the shape of the dinosaur.

Then a man painted a picture.
It shows what the dinosaur looked like.

See for yourself.

Here are the names of the dinosaurs in this book.

Try to read them.

Try to find them in a museum.

Here are the names of the other animals in the book.
They lived at the time of the dinosaurs.
Try to read them.

Starter's **Dinosaurs** words

skeleton
(page 1)

spike
(page 7)

collarbone
(page 8)

horn
(page 8)

back legs
(page 11)

toe
(page 11)

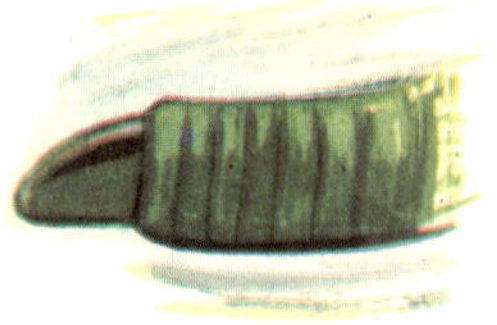

bone
(page 15)

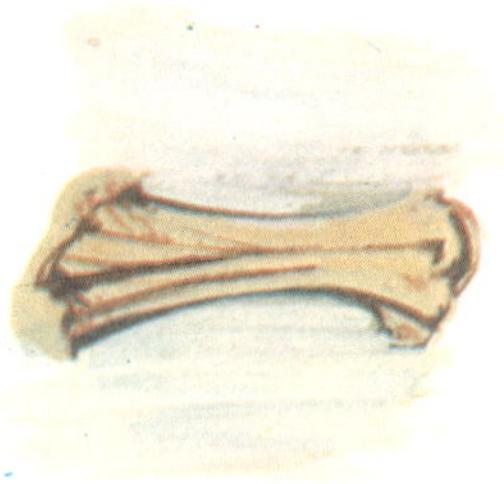

fossil
(page 16)

scientist
(page 18)

museum
(page 19)

LEARNING MATERIALS CENTER
SYLVIA ANGEL, DIRECTOR